know
the
game

Windsurfing

by Wilma Steverink and Wim Thijs

The publisher would like to stress that a
buoyancy aid should always be worn when
windsurfing, and to recommend the use of a
wetsuit in cool climates.

Published by A & C Black (Publishers) Ltd
35 Bedford Row, London WC1R 4JH

CW00602090

Contents

Foreword

Windsurfing is one of the most exciting concepts in the history of sailing development – a fast, demanding sailing craft which is so light you can carry it under your arm, place it easily on a car roof rack, or even tow it behind your bicycle if you live near a sailing water!

One of the principal attractions of the sailboard is its simplicity and, therefore, low cost compared with even the most basic of sailing dinghies. Its impact on other water sports has been dramatic, for as well as utilising every available piece of sailing water it has attracted water sports enthusiasts away from previously popular activities – dinghy sailing has been particularly hit – and many sailing clubs have encouraged windsurfing sections to maintain club activity and retain their members. Anyone who can swim and is reasonably fit can learn to sail a board.

You will find in this book all the basic information you need to get started, but you can't learn everything from a book! It is essential to get someone experienced to teach you the basic sailing positions and manoeuvres, so, because they have been trained to do just that, go to a Royal Yachting Association recognised school.

If you have any other questions or want to know about certificates of proficiency then the Boardsailing coach at the Royal Yachting Association will be able to help you. Write to the R.Y.A., Victoria Way, Woking, Surrey GU21 1EQ.

About the authors

Authors Wilma Steverink and Wim Thijs come from the top ranks of the windsurfing world, having been involved in windsurfing since its introduction into Holland in 1972. Wilma was the first editor of a popular windsurfing magazine and organises National and International competitions. Wim Thijs was a silver medallist and he and his brother Derk have been in the forefront of the windsurfing development and speed sailing.

Wim has extensive experience of teaching windsurfing to beginners and competition sailors – so you should find the book useful to you after you have mastered the basic skill.

A little history

The early history of the sport in England was influenced by the patent taken out by Hoyle Schweitzer on the Windsurfer principle. After several years of deliberation and appeal the British courts have decided that Windsurfing, from the point of view of the patent, was invented by Peter Chilvers when a 12 year old boy in the 1950s. There is, however, no doubt that we can thank Jim Drake and Hoyle Schweitzer for initiating the sports growth with their 'Windsurfer' boards.

The story goes that in 1962 Jim Drake, an aeronautical

engineer, thought it should be possible to produce a simpler sailing craft. He experimented with kites but it wasn't until 1967 that he met with Hoyle Schweitzer who was considering an idea for attaching a sail to a surfboard to avoid the long paddle out through the surf. The idea grew into the 'Baja' board, with a universal joint, skeg and a timber wishbone, embodying the principles of windsurfing. Soon Hoyle was using polyethylene and had renamed the board a Windsurfer. The business grew and soon the board was being made under licence by a Dutch textile firm in Holland and the sport took off in Europe. There are now millions of boards throughout the world.

The sport was recognised by the International Yacht Racing Union (IYRU) in 1977 and is now an Olympic Sport.

Types of board

Since the early days of the 'Windsurfer' there have been enormous strides forward, much of the impetus coming from the high performance conditions sometimes found in Hawaii.

There are now several types of board on the market and these can be summarised as follows:

a) **Flatboards** are full length boards (3.7 to 3.8 m long) with a flat underwater shape, making them stable and easy to sail. They are excellent for learning, light wind casual

sailing and freestyle. Racing takes place under the Division One rules. There is a large choice of boards available, especially secondhand.

Fig.1 The exhilaration of flatboard sailing.

b) **All round Funboards**—the name is a bit of a misnomer as no board can be suitable for all conditions. In reality the boards can be fun in a moderate breeze, but bristle with footstraps and mast tracks. They are also less stable than the flatboards and therefore not ideal for beginners.

c) **Shortboards**, as the name implies, are short (anything below 3.2 m), require a moderate to fresh wind and are unstable, but in return they are much faster and more manoeuvrable. They are a good second board after a season or more of sailing.

d) **Sinkers** are very short boards and do not support a sailor's weight. To sail them you have to lie in the water and let the sail lift you out. They are for experts only, but capable of delivering speeds of up to 35 mph at their fastest. They are very manoeuvrable, especially in surf. They require a strong breeze to sail.

Fig. 2 Waterstarting a sinker – being lifted out of the water by the wind.

Finally there are two types of specialist racing boards:

(i) The Division II board, a lightweight round hulled racing board for use in the top IYRU regattas.

(ii) Course Racing Boards which are long lightweight boards for fast reaching races in strong winds, generally used in World Cup racing (see later).

The sail

Sails have also developed considerably over the last few years, becoming much more manageable, especially in strong winds. The more sophisticated sails such as RAF Camber induced sails imitate an aircraft wing to provide lift and so speed. Those new to the sport should ignore these and look for a 'Fun Sail' of between 5.4 and 6.0 sq.m depending on your size and weight. If they have battens there should only be one or two full length ones at the top and possibly two or three down the leech. A sail with a short boom makes the learning process much easier, (about 2.0 m is ideal).

Your local dealer will be delighted to help you choose suitable equipment, and should be able to arrange a demonstration.

Rigging the board

Clever people will, of course, spend an afternoon finding out exactly how a sailboard fits together before taking to the water with it. What parts does a sailboard have, what are they for and what can you do with them?

The board

The board is made of a tough material such as polyethylene, polyester, ABS, or, in the more expensive boards, epoxy.

The shell is pumped full of foam which strengthens the board and gives buoyancy in the event of damage. The top of the board is roughened slightly so that the feet do not slip on it when it is wet. The underside of the board must be smooth for minimum resistance in the water. In the middle of the board is a slot for the removable daggerboard or rotating centreboard (the daggerboard slot) and on the bottom at the rear is a fitment for the skeg or fin. Make sure the skeg points backwards when you fit it. When inserted on the board, the daggerboard also points backwards. On top, in front of the daggerboard slot, you will find the mast step slot, hole or track in which the mast foot is inserted.

The mast foot

This is the most ingenious part of the sailboard. The bottom part is inserted into the mast step, while the top fits into the lower end of the mast. Between the two parts is the universal joint, which allows the mast to be turned in all directions. If the mast is not held upright it immediately falls on to the water.

The mast

The mast is usually made of either glass fibre reinforced epoxy resin or aluminium. It is tapered. The bottom of the mast goes over the mast foot, and the top ends in a mast head plug to prevent water penetrating the hollow mast.

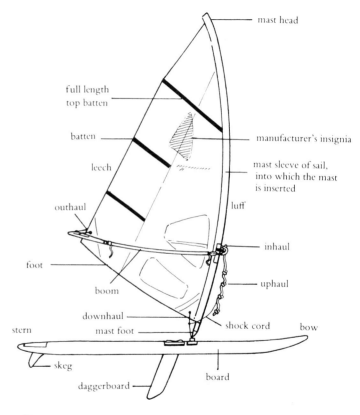

Fig. 3

The daggerboard

This is made of plastic or wood. The leading and trailing edges of the daggerboard are shaped so as to minimize water resistance in the sailing direction. If you look along the cross section of the daggerboard, you will see that the front is rounded and the rear comes to a point. Without a daggerboard the sailboard would be pushed by the wind *and would simply drift off in the direction of the wind*. The daggerboard counteracts this sideways drifting of the board. When you stand on the board and the wind blows into the sail, the daggerboard with its large surface area will prevent the board from drifting away from the wind and help the board to move in the sailing direction. When fitted in its slot, the daggerboard must point to the rear (with the rounded edge to the front).

The boom

The boom consists of two curved parts joined at each end; the sail fits between the two. You hold the mast and sail by the boom when sailing and you use it to steer the sailboard. Originally the boom was made of curved layers of teak glued together, but is now of aluminium, lined with rubber or textile material for a good grip. The uphaul, with which you can lift the sail from the water, is attached to the front of the boom.

The sail

The sail is made of polyester fabric or, on the more expensive sails, Mylar. Both materials are resistant to moisture and sunlight. The sail has batten pockets into which battens fit which serve to stiffen and support the leech.

If you want to fold up the sail, always let it dry on the mast first. It is unwise to allow it to flap in the wind as this pulls the stitching and ruins the sail. Take out the battens and fold the sail so that there are no folds in the windows. Some people roll the sail round the mast if they intend to go out on the water again soon. Make sure that the 'downhaul' is released if you intend to store the sail in this way. Check the stitches regularly; minor repairs are quickly done with a needle and thread and prevent big tears.

Rigging

1 Check that the mast head fits into the mast; wrap some adhesive tape round it if necessary.
2 Insert the mast into the sail's *mast sleeve* from the bottom.
3 There are many methods of attaching the boom to the mast and the most important factor is achieving a good fit to the mast. Most manufacturers have their own methods.

We illustrate one popular method here.

Make a clove hitch round the mast (see Fig. 4) with the *inhaul*, which is a nylon cord. Now draw the end of the

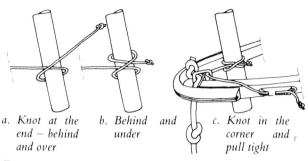

a. Knot at the end – behind and over   b. Behind and under   c. Knot in the corner and pull tight

Fig. 4 Clove hitch

The inhaul should preferably be brought along behind the mast once more. The line then runs from the clove hitch to the boom, back to the mast, behind and along (above the clove hitch) to the boom and only then through the V-clip. A clove hitch with an extra turn in front is often recommended, but this has the disadvantage that it is practically impossible to undo. If properly positioned and firmly tightened, a simple clove hitch is perfectly satisfactory.

inhaul through the eye in the broom (at the front), pull tight and fix it in the front cleat on one side of the boom (Fig. 4).
4 Attach the *mast foot* to the mast (in some types the mast foot is fixed to the mast) and tie the mast foot and the sail together with the *downhaul* (another nylon cord). You can use a flat knot, or a knot of your own.

The downhaul is also known as the luff tensioner because the luff of the sail can be stretched really tight with it. The *luff* is the front edge of the sail.

5 Attach the outer end of the sail to the rear of the boom with the *outhaul*. Pass the outhaul through the eye or ring at the rear of the boom, through the sail eye and back to the boom. If required, the ends of the outhaul can be prevented from pulling out of the cleats on the boom with a knot.
6 Fit the *safety line* between the mast foot and the board; this prevents the sail from separating from the board in a strong wind, an essential safety feature.
7 Check that the mast foot fits firmly into the board. It must not come loose when the sail is eventually rigged. (At the beginning, however, you must also make sure it is not too tight a fit in the board, as you might sometimes get pinned between the board and the mast if the latter falls down. The mast foot then has to come loose easily.)
8 The daggerboard is inserted when the sailboard is in the water, unless it is a fully retractable type, in which case you should fit it on shore.

Hopefully you have not forgotten to fit the skeg on the underside of the board at the rear.
9 The entire assembly of the mast/mast foot/sail/boom is called the *rig*. Attach the *uphaul* to the front of the boom and tie it with shock cord to the mast foot or downhaul.

Practical windsurfing

As stated in the preface, we do not intend to send you out on to the water with this book alone as a guide. But you should read it carefully before taking lessons, and use it afterwards for reference.

Learning at a boardsailing school is much faster (and safer) than trying to do it by yourself, one reason being that schools have simulators. These are sailboards on land which, because they are mounted on a clever mechanism, simulate the behaviour of the board on the water. With a simulator you can practise with sail and board without every mistake being punished immediately with a ducking! But every mistake can be very effectively pointed out and corrected by the instructor, who stands right next to you. In this way you learn the principles of windsurfing very quickly and thoroughly, whereas starting off by practising on the water will turn out to be more of a training in swimming. The instructor will be invaluable on the water as well. You don't only have to learn by bitter experience. The instructor will help you to analyse your mistakes. He will tell you the points to which you must devote particular attention (some things are difficult for all beginners, but there are big individual differences).

Also, it is safer to learn at a school! The first time you go out on the water, you forget everything all around you – it is so fascinating. That always happens at the beginning and can of course be very dangerous. The instructor watches out and sees that all goes smoothly, so that you have an enjoyable and constructive day.

One word of warning about sailing and that is, never go out when the wind is offshore, because you are sheltered on shore and therefore underestimate the wind strength. The rescue services frequently have to help windsurfers who have drifted out to sea, because they went out in an offshore wind.

We follow a *typical school method*, to prepare you for what awaits you at the school. We leave out practising on the simulator, in which all the actions that we shall describe on the water are first performed on land.

Balancing exercises on the board

Carrying the board to the water is very easy if you turn it on its side and hold it by the daggerboard slot on each side. A board weighs about 20 kilos and that is easy enough to carry. Put the board in the water, insert the daggerboard (providing the water is deep enough!) and then start finding out how it feels to climb on to a board and stand on it. The sail stays on the shore; you are dealing with the board, and that is enough at present. At first the board will feel very wobbly, as if it only wanted to tip you into the water. Carefully step forward as far as you can, turn round and then go back as far as possible. Repeat this a few times. Kneel in the middle of the board and let it rock from side to side. Also test the stability of the board while you stand with your legs apart near the daggerboard slot. Try to turn through 360° on the board with small steps.

When you can do all this skilfully, you can go back to the shore to pick up the rig (mast/sail/boom).

Because the sail is unfurled, you run the risk of the wind tearing it out of your hands if you do not carry the rig properly. Lift the rig up above your head with the mast at right angles to the wind and the front of the boom pointing into the wind (Fig. 5). Cast the rig into the water and fit the mast foot firmly into the board. As you get better you will learn beach starting, when you push the board into the water with the rig attached.

Setting the sail

Take a look round before you climb onto the board and check out where the wind is coming from. This you can tell from a flag or trees or just by feel. Now, before you step on to the board, turn it at right angles to the wind, making sure that the sail is on the downwind side of the board. The mast now forms an approximate right angle to the board.

Climb on board, placing your hands over the centreline of the board, the front hand near the mast and the rear over the daggerboard. (We call the hand at the bow end the front hand.) Pull yourself onto the board keeping your bodyweight over the centreline (Fig. 6). You should now be kneeling over the centreline, with your back to the wind. Find the uphaul (Fig. 7). As the sail is full of water, this will give you stability. Stand up with your back to the wind and your feet placed on either side of the mast about shoulder width apart, with your weight distributed equally between them.

Fig. 5 Carrying the rig to the water.

9

Bend your knees and grip the uphaul with your arms outstretched (Fig. 8). Then straighten your legs and use your bodyweight to pull the rig partially clear of the water (the photographs show the right and wrong way to do this Figs. 9 and 10). Pull the rig clear of the water by working hand over hand up the uphaul (Fig. 11). Grasp the mast below the boom with the front or both hands, keeping your arms extended. You should now be standing with your back to the wind, knees very slightly bent, with the board at right angles to the wind and the sail fluttering. This is known as the Secure Position, and you should be comfortable and stable holding this position (Fig. 12).

Then, still holding the mast, move it carefully towards the front of the board (the *bow*) and you will see how the front of the board turns away from the wind. If you move the mast towards the back of the board (the *stern*) the front of the board will turn up into the wind. In this way you can make the board stay at right angles to the wind. Now turn the board a few times through 180° under the sail, both clockwise and anticlockwise. (See Figs. 13 to 16.)

To start sailing you should come back to the Secure Position, and establish a goal point, checking for obstructions in the way (Fig. 17). Grasp the mast with the front hand, and move the back foot over the daggerboard case, keeping yourself over the centreline of the board. Move the front foot behind the mast near the centreline and pointing forwards. Maintain the board and rig at 90° to each other using the front hand (Fig. 18). You are now in the Start Position.

Climbing on board

Fig. 6 Climb on board, placing your hands over the centreline of the board.

Fig. 7 Kneel on the centreline and find the uphaul for stability.

Fig. 8 Stand up using the uphaul for balance.

Fig. 9 Stand up, bending your knees slightly, and use your bodyweight to pull the rig partially clear of the water.

Fig. 10 The wrong method of pulling up the sail – the back is bent, which could cause damage.

Fig. 11 Work hand over hand up the uphaul.

Secure Position

Fig. 12 Grasp the mast below the boom with your front or both hands, arms extended – this is the 'Secure Position' from which all manoeuvres start when you are learning. (The board is at right angles to the rig with the sail downwind – the wind is coming from the left.)

Turning the board through 180°

Fig. 13 *Hold the mast and move towards the front of the board letting the rig swing back.*

Fig. 14 *The board will start turning slowly. Keep shuffling round the front of the mast, turning the board.*

Fig. 15 Keep moving round until you reach the 'Secure Position'.

Fig. 16 Back to 'Secure Position' facing the other direction.

Fig. 17 Start from the Secure Position.

Fig. 18 Move the back foot over the daggerboard case and front foot behind the mast. Pull the rig over to the position where it becomes balanced.

Fig. 19 A side view showing the sail in the balance position. Rest your back hand on the boom.

Fig. 20 Move your front hand to the boom. The rig should still be flapping.

Fig. 21 Sheeting in is achieved by pulling in with the back hand and sailing off.

Turn to face the direction in which you are going and pull the rig, using your front hand on the mast, over to the position where it balances and becomes light. You should be able to see the front of the board through the sail window. Rest your back hand on the boom (Fig. 19) and move your front hand from the mast to the boom (Fig. 20). To start moving pull in with the back hand to fill the sail with wind, at the same time transferring your weight to the back foot. This is the sailing position (Fig. 21).

This should be a smooth flowing movement, and you must remember that your body weight balances the power which the rig generates as the rig is pulled in. This must be taken increasingly by the back foot as the power increases. The other point to watch for is the front of the sail flapping, which often happens because you have not pulled the rig over to the balance point. The front of the sail should be full at all times whilst sailing.

Stopping is a matter of returning to the Secure Position when the sail should always be lowered gently into the water.

Steering

In the Secure Position we practised moving the mast towards the bow and the stern. If we now do this with both hands, we can bring about a change of course. When the board is in the water, with the daggerboard fitted, the board is in effect *fixed* in the water by the daggerboard. The board may be compared to a revolving door, with the daggerboard acting as a *pivot* about which it runs. If you press against the door in the middle near the pivot it will not turn. But if, for example, you push on the left, the door will turn to the right. It is exactly the same with the board on the water. (See Fig. 29 on page 24.)

Luffing up (towards the wind)

Identify a new goal point and draw the rig across the body, leaning the rig towards the back of the board and making sure that the position of the sail relative to the wind does not change. Once again, the sail must not flap immediately aft of the mast. The board will luff up – i.e. the front of the board will turn into the wind (Fig. 22). To stop turning, bring the sail back to its former position and keep the back hand fairly taut so as to continue to catch the wind. (Again watch the sail just aft of the mast.)

Bearing away

Draw the rig across the body, inclining the mast forwards and to windward, extending the front arm (Fig. 23). The board will then bear away – i.e. the front of the board will turn away from the wind. To stop turning, we bring the sail back to its former position. Again see that the sail does not flap. The board will then follow a straight course in the new direction.

Fig. 22 Luff up by pulling the rig across the body and leaning it backwards. The board luffs up to the left (out of the picture).

Fig. 23 Extend the front arm to bear away (to the right in this picture).

Tacking

Sailing is exciting, but you get further and further away from the place where you started. You have to get back, but how? For this purpose you must turn the board through 180° (a process called *tacking*). Start by luffing up (tilt the mast towards the back of the board until you are almost head to wind). Now transfer the front hand to the mast, then move the front foot ahead of it. Step in front of the mast, transferring the back hand to it. Shuffle slowly round the mast keeping your weight central and leaning the rig towards the back until you can resume the Secure Position, then sail off as before. Make sure the movements flow and the sail doesn't fill from the wrong side.

The secret of tacking lies in practising the various operations smoothly in the correct order. Start slowly and speed up as you improve.

Gybing

Start by bearing away (i.e. rake the mast forward) until you feel the wind coming from diagonally behind you. Let go of the boom with the back hand and take hold of the mast. Now grip the mast with the back hand, move it to rotate the board to the Secure Position, and sail off. Once again the new direction of sailing is 180° to the old one. (See Figs. 24 to 27.)

Gybing

Fig. 24 Bear away until you feel . . .

Fig. 25 . . . the wind coming from behind.

Fig. 26 Grip the mast with the back hand and rotate the board . . .

Fig. 27 . . . to the Secure Position.

Main points

The following are the most important points to bear in mind when sailing on a sailboard:

- when you set the sail, see that the board is at right angles to the wind and that you stand with your back to the wind;
- when you want to start sailing, the sail must be at right angles to the board and flap in the wind; it must be completely out of the water;
- you must always keep the front hand in position on the boom above the front foot, except to steer;
- if you have to let go of the sail for any reason, always let go with the back hand first;
- when steering (luffing up and bearing away), the position of the sail relative to the wind must not change; the sail must remain *full of wind*, almost (but not quite) flapping;
- emergency stop: you can bring your sailboard to a halt immediately by simply dropping the sail, jumping off and holding on to the board.

Fig. 28 ***Practice circle*** *for beginners (you can of course go round in the opposite direction).*

You can see from this circle when you have to tack and when you must gybe. The more experienced you are, the faster you can start off again after tacking or gybing. Beginners must first go on turning until they reach the correct starting position (see drawing).

Tacking: start by luffing up – the stern turns under the sail
Gybing: start by bearing away – the bow turns under the sail

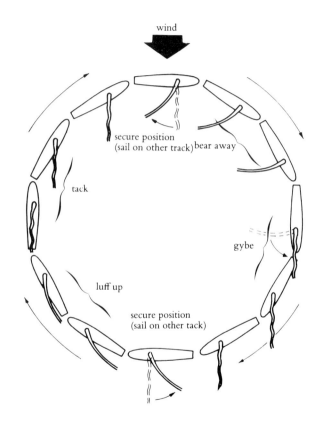

wind

secure position
(sail on other track) bear away

tack

gybe

luff up

secure position
(sail on other track)

Theory of windsurfing

Definitions

The sailing world has a language of its own. When you are driving, on land, you 'turn left', 'turn right', 'go round a corner'; there are no direct equivalents of these manoeuvres on the water. It may seem confusing, but the situation on the water is after all not the same as in a town with roads, round-abouts and traffic lights. The water is a single open expanse, but here too there are rules of the road, which we shall consider in more detail in the section on safety. Let us start with the simple things.

The right-hand side of the board, looking from the stern towards the bow, is called the *starboard side*. The left-hand side is the *port side*. We have already told you that the front of the board is called the *bow* and the back the *stern*.

In relation to your board the side from which the wind is blowing is the *windward* or *weather* side and the other is the *leeward*. It follows that any shore on your *leeward* side is a *lee* shore. If you allow yourself to be blown onto that shore it is difficult to get off it. However, that is an aside to the actual business of sailing your board.

Turning the front of the board, the bow, into the wind until the board's head points precisely into the wind is called *luffing up*, while turning it away from the wind is termed *bearing away*. If the turning movement is continued further, we then have the manoeuvres of *tacking* and *gybing* respectively.

A board which is not engaged in a gybing or tacking manoeuvre is said to be *on a tack*. You are sailing either on starboard tack or port tack according to the windward side.

Steering, bearing away and luffing up

When the board is in the water, with the daggerboard fitted, the board will pivot laterally about the daggerboard. If the point at which the daggerboard acts is imagined to be fixed, obviously any force which is applied to the board at the end will make it turn. (See paragraph on Steering, page 18.)

Now, of course, it makes no difference whether we push against the board or the wind pushes the sail above it. The force of the wind can be imagined to act at one point in the sail, the centre of effort. If the centre of effort is kept above the

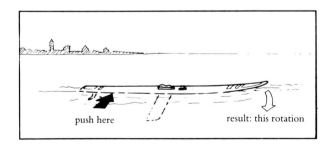

push here   result: this rotation

Fig. 29 The board as a revolving door (see page 18)

daggerboard the board will not turn; it is balanced. If, however, the centre of effort is moved aft of the daggerboard a turning effect will result. The front of the board will turn up into the wind.

So, leaning the rig towards the back of the board results in luffing up (Fig. 30).

If, on the other hand, the centre of effort is moved forward of the daggerboard, by leaning the rig towards the front of the board, then you are bearing away (Fig. 31).

As soon as you want to sail straight again after a course correction, you set the sail straight up above the daggerboard, taking up the sailing position with the front hand vertically above the front foot. The board then stops turning and sails straight on.

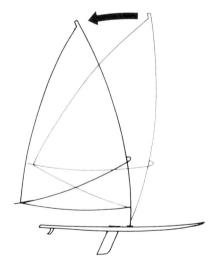

Fig. 30 Luffing up

Fig. 31 Bearing away

Fig. 32 Sailing close to the wind.

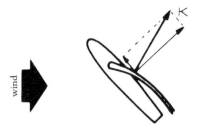

Why can a board sail – diagonally at least – against the wind? If you set sail on dry land and put one foot on the mast foot, we can perform an instructive experiment. You need a steady, gentle wind. Just pull in your back hand a little. The sail will set nicely. Now bring your hands closer together. Finally, let go with one hand and move the other backwards and forwards until the sail is precisely in balance. In what direction is the force acting? You will feel that it is approximately perpendicular to the surface of the sail! Fig. 32 is a plan view of a board sailing close to the wind. The drive of the sail (or sail force) is indicated by the arrow K. The sail force acts mainly laterally, but there is also a forward component, which is represented by the dotted lines and arrows. Nevertheless the board will sail forward nicely, as it can be moved very easily in the forward direction. This is due partly to the shape of the board (long and narrow), but mainly to the shape of the daggerboard! The daggerboard moves readily through the water forwards but with extreme difficulty sideways. As a result the powerful lateral push of the sail force has little effect and the small amount of forward thrust a great deal!

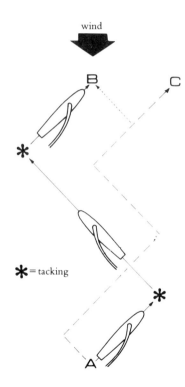

Fig. 33 Sailing against the wind from A to B (or C.)

Tacking and gybing
You will quite often want to sail to a point into the wind e.g. from A to B (or C) in fig. 33.

   You cannot of course sail straight into the eye of the wind. But you can certainly sail diagonally into the wind. Good windsurfers can sail against the wind at an angle of about 45° (see drawing). If you proceed on the port and starboard tacks alternately (by tacking) you can sail to a point directly against the wind.

At first it is difficult to sail diagonally against the wind (close to the wind). But you will realize that this is very important, as you cannot otherwise sail everywhere you want. Even to get back to your starting point you will often have to sail against the wind! You tack in the positions starred in Fig. 33. (Of course, you can sail from A to B by any routes, but you will always have to tack.) The other way, from B to A, you can obviously run straight downwind. However, you could also precisely follow the path shown in the diagram. But in this case you would have to gybe at the stars, instead of tacking!

   So: Changing tack against the wind is tacking
       Changing tack with the wind behind you is gybing.

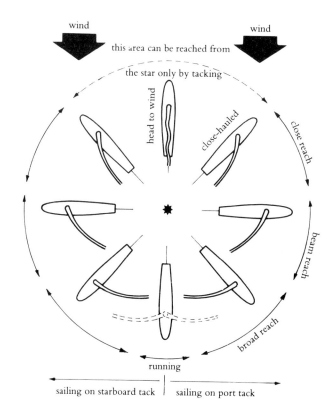

wind   wind

this area can be reached from

the star only by tacking

head to wind

close-hauled

close reach

beam reach

broad reach

running

sailing on starboard tack | sailing on port tack

Fig. 34 The points of sail.

27

Safety

Windsurfing in safety

1 Do not windsurf without a wetsuit unless it is really warm (and the water as well). Always wear a buoyancy aid.

2 The board and rig must be joined by a safety line.

3 Always observe the 'rules of the road'.

4 Avoid water used by commercial craft.

5 Keep away from swimmers and speedboats.

6 Take notice of weather forecasts and keep an eye on the sky.

7 Do not windsurf in nature reserves and water catchment areas.

8 Make sure you know the local regulations.

9 Be careful on water where there are currents.

10 Do not forget that if there is an offshore wind you may have problems getting back. It is best never to go out in offshore winds as the winds increase the further you go out.

11 If you cannot get your rig up fast enough as another craft approaches, leave the sail in the water. Make sure that you are seen – draw attention to yourself by shouting or waving both hands above your head.

12 Beginners should keep close to the shore.

13 Windsurfing at sea is quite dangerous and also harder because of currents, waves and deep trenches in front of beaches. Begin on inland stretches of water.

14 If you intend to go windsurfing for a long time or to take a little trip, tell someone on shore.

15 If the mast separates from the board and the rig drifts off, do not swim after it. Stay on the board and paddle towards the rig.

16 If you get into difficulties, always stay on your board! The board cannot sink. Sit up on the board and give a distress signal by slowly and repeatedly raising and lowering arms outstretched each side. The arms do not rise above the level of the shoulders (i.e. no higher than horizontal) or better still carry a Dayglo flag to wave (available from the RYA).

17 Sometimes you cannot return to the shore by sailing. This may happen because you have overestimated your capabilities with an offshore wind, or because of some mishap; for example, a line breaking. Here is what to do. Sit on the board, withdraw the mast foot from it and detach the shock cord and the outhaul. Then roll up the sail as best you can, starting at the clew. Begin by grasping the reinforced patch and roll the sail as tightly as possible towards the mast; remove the battens and either stick them down the back of your wetsuit or up the mast sleeve; lift the boom to lie alongside the mast, tying the end to the mast with the uphaul; take hold of the uphaul, wind it a few times around the rolled-up sail from the boom upwards and secure it with the elastic and the cleat hook. The entire rig is now a compact unit. Place the trussed-up rig on the board with mast foot pointing forwards. Lie on your stomach on top of the rig and paddle with both hands to the shore (Fig. 35). Paddling

Fig.35 Roll the sail tightly, tie together and lay boom and sail on board. Lie on top of the rig and paddle.

sitting up is usually less effective and practically impossible against anything more than a light wind. Lying on top of the rolled-up rig you can also let youself be towed by another sailboard. The windsurfer must come alongside you, you get hold of his mast foot or daggerboard loop, and away you go! 18 Always carry spare line to repair any minor breakages— you can fix it to the boom out of the way.

Rules of the road

Fig. 36 shows some of the rules of the road. Full rules are given in the booklet *The International Regulations for Preventing Collisions at Sea* (RYA Booklet G2).

For most of the time you will be using your board in enclosed or restricted waters and you should keep clear of larger craft which may only be able to navigate safely in the deeper water of a channel or fairway; these latter may be marked by navigational buoys – usually red and green near harbours.

Since the board is highly manoeuvrable there is no need for you ever to get into close quarters with these larger vessels. Between sailing vessels three rules apply *when they are approaching each other* (Regulations, rule 12).

1. When each has the wind on a different side the one with the wind on its port side keeps out of the way. The one on 'starboard tack' has priority and its sail will be over the left side of it since the wind is coming over the starboard side of it.

2. When both have the wind on the same side, the one to windward keeps out of the way.

3. If you are on port tack (with the wind coming over the left side of your board) and you cannot be certain what tack the other approaching board or boat is on, you keep clear.

When overtaking, the rule states 'any vessel overtaking any other shall keep out of the way of the vessel being overtaken' (see Fig. 36). If you are in any doubt whether you are the overtaking craft, assume that you are until you are past and clear. If you meet a small motor boat, it, being under power, should keep clear of you. In open water 'power gives way to sail' because powered craft are more able to change course quickly and accurately. A cruiser or boat in a narrow channel will normally have right of way, so use your common sense and keep out of trouble.

Whatever you do always make your intentions clear and remember that the rules require you to avoid collision even if the other craft does not do what it should. At all times your conduct afloat should be such that it gives the sport of windsurfing a good name.

Fig. 36 Principal 'rules of the road'.

Power and sail

Your path crosses someone else's: power gives way to sail when in open water.

Two small power boats.

Approaching each other head on: both give way to starboard (right).

Small sailing boat (2 possibilities)

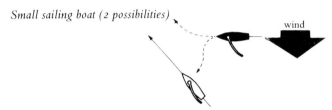

wind

2. Sailing on same tack: windward gives way.

Overtaking

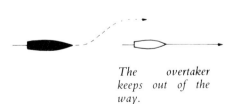

The overtaker keeps out of the way.

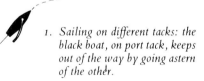

1. Sailing on different tacks: the black boat, on port tack, keeps out of the way by going astern of the other.

Wetsuits and hypothermia

(lowered deep body temperature)

Getting wet is unavoidable when learning to windsurf, and even later everyone is bound to get the odd involuntary ducking. Many people do not realize that an unintentional cold dip of this kind can prove fatal. If you are forced to stay in the water for a long time, you are confronted with the number one danger facing every water sportsman: deep body cooling. This means that the body temperature falls so far that you are bound to die whether or not you are a good swimmer. This is because our bodies cannot easily retain heat. At a water temperature of 20°C the body gives up four or five times as much heat to the water as at the same temperature in free air. To offset heat loss heat production must be increased. Our bodies are capable of producing four or five times as much heat as normal, but not more. It is therefore unavoidable that the body cools very rapidly if the water temperature falls below 20°C. What is so dangerous is that you do not yourself notice that your body is losing heat too rapidly because you become apathetic, hallucinate and get into a state of euphoria if body temperature falls below 30°C.

A wetsuit is certainly essential for windsurfing in most European waters where the temperature hardly ever rises above 20°C even in summer. A wetsuit is specially designed to reduce heat loss. It has a powerful insulating effect, sealing your body heat in. Whatever kind of wetsuit you wear, you will notice that when you fall into the water a thin layer of

Fig. 37 Long John wetsuit with buoyancy aid over.

water trickles into the suit. This is perfectly normal – it is after all a *wet* suit! That staying warm feeling is due to the layer of water between your skin and the suit. The water is warmed by your body. The air bubbles in the rubber of your suit have an insulating effect and prevent this layer of water from in turn giving up heat to the surrounding colder water. For this reason a wetsuit must be a good fit – it must be neither too large nor too small. For a windsurfer, sleeves that are too tight are a disaster, as the arms have a lot to do when there is the slightest bit of wind. The greater the exertion, the more the muscles expand because the circulation is enhanced. If there is no room for the muscles to expand, the blood supply is restricted and you get cramp or become tired.

Most suits are made of synthetic neoprene rubber. Take your time trying on your wetsuit. A dry wetsuit gives you a shut-in feeling – it is stiff and soon starts irritating. Don't worry – that's normal. When the neoprene is wet, it becomes a veritable second skin. There must be enough room under the armpits to move your arms more or less normally in spite of the pressure of the rubber. Watch out for rough patches or edges that chafe the skin. When you eventually get wet, these rough bits can scratch your skin open in a very few minutes. The length of the sleeves and legs is totally unimportant, but make sure the suit is the right length from shoulder to seat. Bend down a few times; the whole thing should not pull. But don't overdo it – a seat that hangs down between your thighs is a disaster and also traps much too much water. Remember that zips left and right are all very well, but zips do not insulate. The fewer zips the better. Each time you use your suit, rinse it clean afterwards.

A number of different types are available: the *shorty*, a one-piece suit with short legs and short sleeves or no sleeves and legs at all; the *long john*, a sleeveless suit with long legs; the *overall*, a one-piece suit with long sleeves and long legs; the *jacket*, which has long sleeves and covers the hips, as well as a flap on the back panel which you bring forward between your legs and fasten to the front panel; the *bolero*, a short jacket with long sleeves often worn together with long johns; and the *pantaloon*, long trousers which extend from the waist to the ankles and are usually combined with a jacket.

The choice is of course a personal one, but the shorty seldom provides enough protection. It is usually bought as an extra to wear on warm days. Long johns are the most commonly used type, usually combined with the bolero. In warm weather long johns will keep you warm enough, and your shoulders and arms can move comfortably. In colder weather you wear a bolero on top, or alternatively a one-piece steamer or drysuit.

Harness

Lovely weather and a Force 5 wind, but after ten minutes your rig sags down on to the water because your arms ache unbearably. You massage your arm muscles, fume at your lack of fitness and cast irritated glances at the people zooming past you cheerfully in the same wind.

But have a good look: hardly any of them are sailing under their own arm power – they are probably using a *harness*. Once you have mastered the harness technique, not only do you save your strength but your brief moments of pure enjoyment join together to produce hours of sailing delight. Even dead tired windsurfers can always get back home using their harness. So why shouldn't every beginner immediately strap himself into a harness? Well, a harness is not entirely without its dangers. You might get caught in a harness line if you fall and a panic may quickly arise if you then end up under the sail. One very common painful tumble is when a sudden gust of wind propels the sail, the sailor and everything else to the lee. You then fall heavily with your rib cage against the boom! So do not start using a harness until you are fairly competent.

The harness can act as a buoyancy aid and should be long enough to transfer the weight to the small of your back. For long distance work some sailors even use a harness to sit in.

Make sure the harness fits well and that the back does not cut into your shoulders or under the armpits. It must be made of tough material as there must not be a double thickness the shoulders. Are there sharp edges on the seams? Th

might chafe most unpleasantly on your bare skin when you wear the harness. The hook should be roughly at the level of the bottom of your breastbone. The metal plate to which the hook is often fixed must have four grooves (on each side), through which the lines can be fed. The opening of the hook may then point upwards or downwards. Some harnesses are now designed with long spreader hooks which, as the name implies, help spread the load on the rib cage. The harness lines must be adjustable in position so that it can be worn on the bare skin or over a life-jacket. As an additional safety measure

Fig. 38 Using a harness which takes the weight of the rig off the arms and allows more sailing time in greater comfort.

it is convenient if the fastening is of the quick release type. Imagine that you are flung off your board, are caught on the harness and get stuck under the sail, unable to release yourself quickly. You just release the harness fastener and quickly take it off.

To allow you to sail with the harness you must attach harness lines to both parts of the boom wishbone. These lines can be made of nylon cord about 6 mm thick and about 1.20 m long. Do not leave too much slack when tying the lines to the boom – remember that when you hook yourself on to the line you will still need your arms for steering the board.

Recently the waist harness and seat harness have been introduced, both very much more comfortable than the chest harness, causing less backache, and permitting lower booms. Techniques of use are very similar, but you may need additional buoyancy.

Harness sailing technique

Practise with the harness on land first, and then go out on the water in a light wind and practise tacking so that you have to release the line from the hook. Practise releasing – take the power of the rig through your arms and disengage the line. If necessary shake the boom to make sure you are free.

If the wind dies and you fall in backwards, you may find yourself under the sail or between the mast and board. Stay calm, let yourself fall, get hold of the hook, detach the harness line and come up again. If there is too much wind and you are thrown into the air, so that you are in danger of spinning round your own harness, release the fastener and take off the harness. All these crazy things will not happen if your technique is good. You will then release promptly and automatically. For experienced windsurfers the harness can only mean extra safety and pleasure.

Insurance

In certain circumstances a sailboard and its equipment can be lethal, such as when it falls off your roof-rack into the path of oncoming traffic, or when someone bumps into it – just two examples of accidents which can happen when the board is not being sailed, and which is often not covered by existing car, household or personal accident policies. To be absolutely sure that you are covered against claims by third parties and theft of the board and wet suits you should take out a special windsurfing policy, either through the Royal Yachting Association if you are a member, or with a marine insurance company. Premiums are about 4% to 5% of the value of the goods insured.

Some sailing waters and most sailing clubs will require evidence of insurance before you can go afloat, so it's in your own interests to arrange the insurance as soon as you buy your equipment. Always remember that it will just as easily fit under someone else's arm if you leave it lying around!

Transport

Carrying the board under your arm is simple enough if you don't have far to go. Hold the board with the top (i.e., the side the mast goes into) towards you. Put one hand over the board into the daggerboard slot and support the board in the mast step slot with the other. The whole thing is in balance and the board can be carried very easily like this. However, if you have a hundred metres or even more to cover, heaving the board along can get very difficult. You can now buy handy little carts – in fact more like a miniframe with two small wheels – to take the hard labour out of this chore.

On the roof of your car

Before you transport your board by car you should make sure that you have the right equipment and check out the situation with your car manual to see whether it can bear the weight. Most car roofs will accept one board, but it is important to know the maximum roof loading for your car.

To transport the board you need 'roof bars'. These are fitted some distance apart on the edge of the roof. If the edge is rusty this can obviously cause lots of trouble.

To provide a soft bed for the board, most windsurfers use pieces of polystyrene or foam plastic. Put the boom on first, then the mast and finally the board itself, with the skeg at the stern pointing aloft.

Fig. 39 Tie boards securely to the roofrack.

Special lines are available for securing the board firmly. The kind of luggage sling normally used on a roof-rack is totally unsuitable. The special slings have a mechanism which clamps the board absolutely solidly. You need two of them. Check that everything really is absolutely firm, including the mast. The mast can, if necessary, be tied to one of the carriers with an extra small line. There is no limit to the possible damage if the roof load should come loose and slide off. Make sure, too, that you obey the traffic regulations. With small cars such as a Mini or a Fiat 600 the mast will project too far to the rear. So tie a red rag to the projection and put a red light on it at night. It is a good idea to tie the board to the front and rear bumpers.

Young people who do not yet have a driving licence can, if they are at all skilled with their hands, knock together a small cart to tow behind their bike. This is of course inappropriate if you live in a busy town, as it is certainly inadvisable to weave through traffic with a sailboard behind your bicycle.

A trailer of this kind can be made from two old bicycle wheels with mudguards, four 1-metre angle irons, a long beam to the parcel carrier (the mast can also be used for this) about 2.5 metres long, a piece of carpet to protect the board, a rear light, two reflectors (red and white), and some means of attaching the trailer to the bike's parcel carrier. You will, of course, also need some nuts and bolts and a drill.

In this do-it-yourself project, make sure you observe the traffic regulations applicable to a device of this kind.

Do not forget to provide the rear end of the mast with a nice red rag.

Tricks and games with the board

Freestyle

This is acrobatics on the board; the highest form of interaction between the sailboard and the sailor. It involves perfect control of the board and a precise feeling for how the board responds to every action.

Over one hundred different freestyle tricks are known. It would be beyond the scope of this book to describe them all here, but we can at least help you on the way. Since the Americans invented and developed these tricks, they also originated the names by which they are known worldwide. For most people the first experiment is *railride*. Here you sail with the board on its side and you stand or sit on the upturned side. This is how it's done: When sailing close-hauled on smooth water, flip the lee side of the board into the water with one foot while lifting the windward side of the board out of the water with the other. When you feel the board capsizing, place the windward foot on the daggerboard, as close in as possible to the bottom of the board. To make matters easier, you can let the mast rest against the board. Once you have a perfect command of the trick, this will no longer be necessary. The best exponents of this trick can tack and gybe on the rail (Fig. 40).

Two other classical tricks are the *head dip* and the *nose dip*. Before attempting these, it is advisable first to learn to sail by feel – i.e., without looking at the sail.

The *head dip* is quite easy if you have at least a minimum of

Fig. 40 Railriding.

control over the board in a fresh wind. When you are sailing nicely all you have to do is to lean right back, bending your head back until it touches the water. More skill is needed for the *nose dip*. You start by standing with your back to the sail, your hands holding the boom behind your back. Now bend forward as far as you can and try to touch the water with your nose.

Sitdown and liedown are very impressive to the spectator but not really difficult. All kinds of variations on these can be imagined, a remarkable example being the *foothold*: sailing lying down on the board while manoeuvring the boom with your feet.

Sailing to leeward is another basic exercise. You tack while remaining on the same side of the sail. You can force the sail to the windward with your arms or back while you yourself stand on the lee side. This trick can be followed by a *duck tack*, in which you duck under the boom when tacking.

Taking windsurfing further

There are several options open once you have mastered the basics: racing, high wind sailing, and competition or just plain cruising. One of the most spectacular facets of the latest high wind short boards are the new forms of competition which they have initiated.

Fig. 41 Jenna de Rosnay, a speed-record holder.

present this is over 32 knots for boards; the only sailing craft which is faster is Crossbow, a special 60 ft catamaran.

Another form of competition based initially on the Hawaiian Pan Am Cup is the World Manufacturers Sailboard Association (WMSA), who provide a competition in three disciplines to find the best high wind sailors. Skill, equipment and speed are the vital ingredients which make this a good spectator sport. The racing only takes place if there is a moderate breeze. The three disciplines are as follows:

Course Racing: a triangle race with short beats and long reaches, with the accent on gybing rather then tacking. Tactics are vital, as is the specialist equipment.

Slalom Racing: a reaching race set round several buoys set down the beach. There is plenty of gybing and fast action close in. Races only take a few minutes.

Wave Sailing: basically freestyle in the waves. Sinkers are used for jumping, wave riding and gybing. Many people, however, just wave ride for the exhilaration of the sport.

Possibly the most specialised is speedsailing. Administered by the RYA, competitors have their average speed calculated between two accurately laid out points about 500 m apart. At

Local clubs, regional and national events are held on these principles although the Slalom course is sometimes set round two buoys only.

Fig. 42 Approaching a gybe mark during a slalom race.

Fig. 44 Beating during a race